TOR

CW00662776

TORNADO

IAN BLACK

Airlife

England

ACKNOWLEDGEMENTS

Having produced *Lightning* for Airlife in the Autumn of 1988, it seemed logical to follow with *Tornado*, having converted to the latter in July 1988. The book itself is not intended to be a concise history of the aircraft, detailing each individual mark and unit. It is more a pot-pourri of colourful and unusual photographs.

Many people have helped in the preparation of this book and to them I extend my thanks, in particular Jane Harvey of Canon Cameras. All photographs were taken using Canon and Bronica equipment, using lenses from 16mm to 500mm. Kodak film was used throughout.

Copyright © Ian Black, 1990

First published in the UK in 1990
by Airlife Publishing Ltd.

British Library Cataloging in Publication Data available.

ISBN 1 85310 157 5 (Hardback)
ISBN 1 85310 160 5 (Paperback)

All rights reserved. No part of this book may be reproduced or transmitted in any form or by any means, electronic or mechanical including photocopying, recording or by any information storage and retrieval system, without permission from the Publisher in writing.

Airlife Publishing Ltd.

101 Longden Road, Shrewsbury SY3 9EB, England.

INTRODUCTION

The tri-national Panavia Tornado fighter-bomber has one of the most complex origins of any post-war aircraft. In the United Kingdom the Tornado has basically replaced the RAF's post-war jet bomber force, a move which by the early 1970s was long overdue. Originally, the TSR 2 was to be the British Aircraft Corporation's answer to a 'Multi Role Combat Aircraft' but sadly this project was cancelled on 6 April 1965. Numerous aircraft developed from the cancellation of this project, some of which never left the drawing board. The Buccaneer and Jaguar were ordered by the RAF, as was the American swing wing F111, although this was cancelled at a late stage.

By the late 1960s numerous nations had an urgent need to replace ageing strike aircraft. By July 1970 a tri-national consortium comprising three well known aircraft manufacturers had evolved. These were British Aerospace, Messerschmitt-Bolkow-Blohm (MBB) and Aeritalia, all of which came under the collective title of Panavia, whose Munich offices retained overall control of the project.

As the name 'Multi Role Aircraft' implies, the Tornado was designed to fulfil the roles of various well known tactical aircraft, including Starfighters, Vulcans, Canberras and Buccaneers in the strike role, Jaguars and Starfighters in the reconnaissance role and Phantoms and Lightnings in the air defence role. The engine for the Tornado, the RB199, began airborne flight trials in 1973 mounted under an all-white Vulcan which had previously been used to test Concorde's Olympus engines.

The first prototype Tornado flew on 14 August 1974 at MBB's South German factory at Manching. Second to fly was P02 which flew on 30 October 1974 from Warton in Lancashire. Within two years eight prototypes were flying, with the first Italian aircraft flying on 5 February 1977. With so much flight test work to be completed, it was a remarkable achievement that the RAF's first production GR1 flew from Warton on 7 July 1979.

Initially, aircraft were delivered to the Tri-National Tornado Training Establishment (TTTE) at Cottesmore in the UK. Here aircrew from all four air arms which operate the Tornado receive initial groundschool and basic flying

In an effort to save fuel for its low level mission, *ZA550 JD* of 27 Squadron transits the upper air space where fuel consumption is reduced.

instruction. The aircraft are a mixture of British, German and Italian machines, normally flown without armament. Often pilots and navigators from differing nations are crewed together for their course, flying any one of the three nation's airframes. On completion of the TTTE, RAF crews proceed to RAF Honington to the TWCU Tornado Weapons Conversion Unit for specific weapon training.

The RAF also saw the need in the early 1970s to replace its Lightnings and Phantoms in the Air Defence Role. The replacement aircraft would need to be a long range interceptor capable of protecting the large UK airspace. Maintaining an eighty per cent commonality with the GR1, the ADV Defence Variant's most obvious difference is the longer forward fuselage (4 feet 6 inches). This increases internal fuel capacity and allows the carriage of up to four semi-active Skyflash missiles semi-recessed beneath the .fuselage.

The first of three ADV prototypes, A01, flew on 27 October 1979 from Warton, and has since been used for handling trials and missile clearance tests throughout the entire flight envelope. The RAF accepted the first two ADVs on 5 November 1984. These initial aircraft were substantially different from the F3s now in operational service. The original aircraft were designated F2s and lacked the Ferranti twin inertial navigation system and were fitted with the short RB199 Mk 103 engines. Although both the ADV and GR1 are similar in handling terms, all conversion on to the F3 is undertaken by 229 OCU at RAF Conningsby. The latest Tornado to enter service is the ECR (Electronic Combat Reconnaissance) version designed for use by the West German Air Force, with the possibility of the Italians converting sixteen of their existing aircraft to this standard. The thirty-five new build aircraft will be based at GAF Jever from February 1990.

Overseas deliveries so far have been restricted to the Royal Saudi Arabian Air Force, who have ordered both the ground attack and air defence versions. By early 1990 Tornado production was set to exceed the 1,000 mark, ensuring that the aircraft will be a familiar sight in NATO skies for many years to come.

Opposite: *ZE 832* climbs into the blue. 23 Squadron began to re-equip with Tornado F3s in October 1988, having previously flown Phantom FGR2s from RAF Mount Pleasant airfield situated on the Falkland Islands.

Below: Jabo 31 44+00 in its thirty-year jubilee colours. Jabo 31 are based at Norvenich in central West Germany.

Overleaf: 229 OCU (Operational Conversion Unit) line. The black sooty marks on the fin are caused by the reverse thrust buckets throwing forward the jet efflux across the rear fuselage.

Opposite: Exercise 'Elder Joust', October 1989. Keeping this Victor K2 tanker busy, four 11 Squadron Tornado F3s take on fuel.

Below: Mass line up of German Marine Tornado GR 1s from MFG 1 at Schleswig. The aircraft's normal weapon load is the Kormoran anti-ship missile.

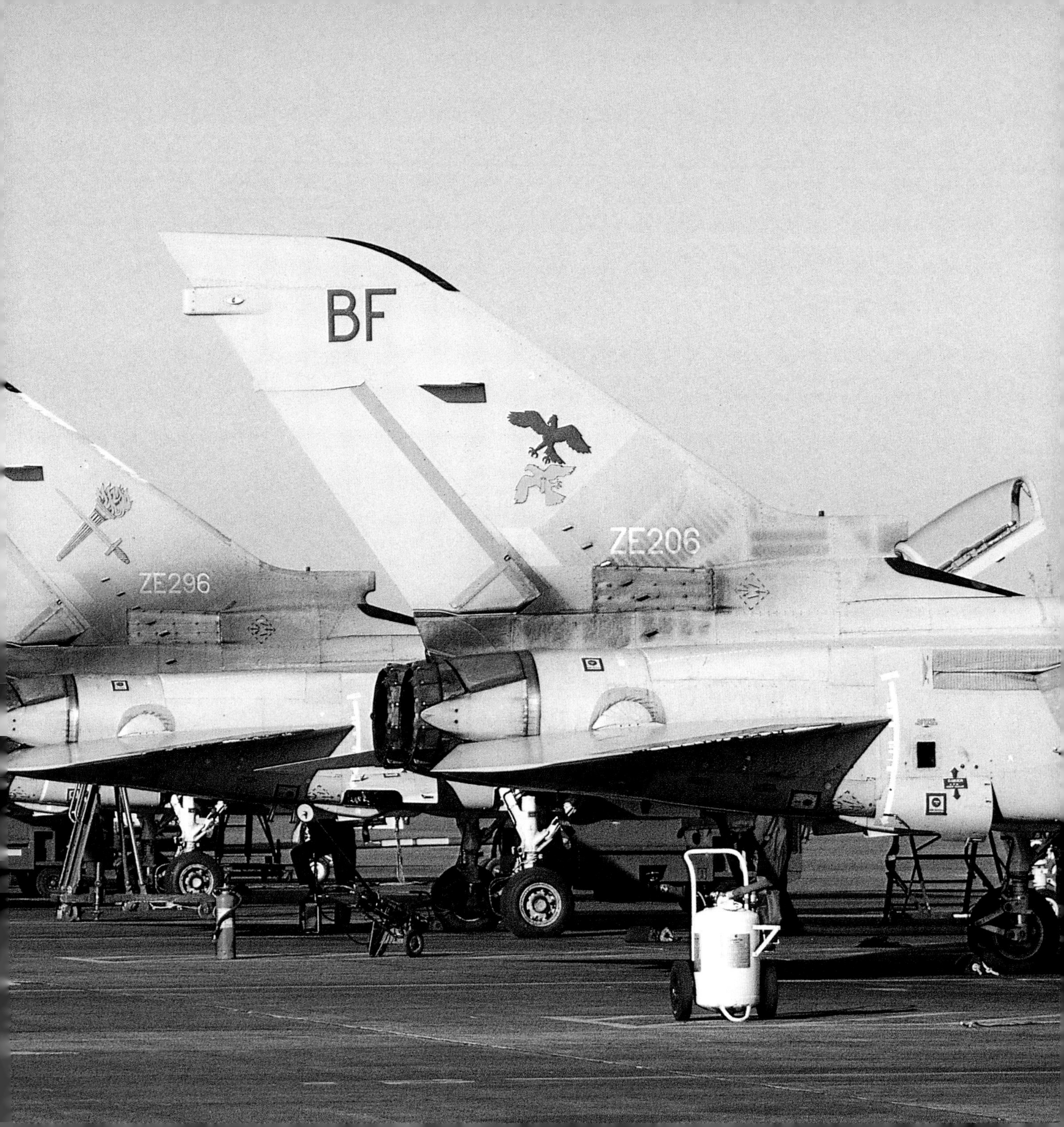
BF
ZE206
ZE296

Opposite: Fish-eye view of the Tornado F3 cockpit and crew.

Below: Close view of a 23 Squadron Tornado F3, the sun glinting off the 23mm single Mauser gun housed internally on the forward right side of the air defence machines. The gun is a remarkably accurate device, with several pilots achieving scores of 100% in air-to-air gunnery.

Overleaf: Ten minutes into a ten hour-plus sortie, two Royal Saudi Air Force Tornado F3s begin their long delivery flight from the British Aerospace factory at Warton in Lancashire. Each aircraft carries two 2,250 litre fuel tanks to reduce the number of air-to-air refuelling contacts between UK and Saudi Arabia.

Opposite: Winter over the North Yorkshire Moors.
(Photograph S. Black)

Below: 9 Squadron, one of the RAF's most famous Bomber Squadrons, painted AZ in a special 75th anniversary colour scheme. 9 Squadron was originally formed at RAF Honnington with the Tornada GR 1, but now operates from RAF Bruggen on the Dutch-German border.

Overleaf: D-T, 11 Squadron's dual control trainer — hence the 'T' code. *ZE786* was delivered to RAF Leeming in May 1988. Seen here taking on fuel from an aircraft of a different era, the Handley Page Victor K2, 55 Squadron are the last Victor operators in the world.

Opposite: Having hit a large bird whilst flying at low altitude, D-B, a 31 Squadron Tornado GR 1 is diverted to RAF Leeming as a precautionary measure. Engine changes on the Tornado are relatively straightforward — this aircraft was airborne within twenty-four hours.

Below: Brand new Tornado F3 EE of 23 Squadron with around twenty-five flying hours on the clock.

Opposite: Low flying over a flat Lincolnshire landscape, *ZE836* has its wings spent at 45 degrees, used for medium speed flight above 450 knots. Skimming across the fields below are the shadows of E-E and the photo ship.

Below: Side shot of the shiny new Tornado F3, *2906*. Two others are visible in the background.

Opposite: 17(F) Squadron, the 'Black Knights', have adopted a special paint scheme on 'C-Z' for their 75th Anniversary, in February 1990.

Below: German prototype 98+06 with intake guards fitted to avoid foreign object damage during engine ground runs.

Opposite: Post gun-firing, the armourers service the Mauser gun prior to the next mission. Spent cases are retained in the spent links bay to the left of the main gun body under the open panel. After only a few days' firing, each aircraft's nose gets blacker and blacker with carbon deposits.

Below: G-D of 20 Squadron at ultra low level, 100 feet above the ground. Only specially trained ground attack pilots are allowed to fly this low in peace time. Specific uninhabited areas are used to train in — desolate parts of Canada are used for this purpose to avoid noise disturbance. A bomber flying at 100 feet presents a particularly difficult target to air defence crews.

Opposite: 2 Squadron based at Laarbruch, have for many years been in the unusual position of being neither a fighter nor a bomber squadron. Previous aircraft have included Hunter, Phantom and the Jaguar in the elite photo recce role. As the aircraft are based in Germany, stencilling is always in dual languages.

Below: German Tornado PO 7 98+06 seen in 1976 liberally covered in dayglo patches for test purposes.

Opposite: Waiting to plug in, four Saudi Tornado F3s await their turn to take fuel from a Tristart Tanker. Not visible is the single point refuelling hose located under the wide bodied Tanker's fuselage. Compared to other aircraft, in-flight refuelling the Tornado F3 is a fairly straightforward affair, the probe being located on the front left side of the aircraft forward of the cockpit.

Below: In an effort to make aircraft more conspicuous at low level, a handful of Tornado GR 1s received brightly coloured fins, red and also white. EA from XV(15) Squadron manages to retain its squadron identity though.

Opposite: A Dambusters Tornado GR 1 showing its wrap around camouflage, not used to advantage over an ice-white sky.

Below: AS 62, a single stick Tornado F3 destined for the Royal Air Force, is rolled off the factory floor in its bright yellow/green primer undercoat.

Bottom: Having completed their annual gun firing camp, six Tornado F3s from 5 Squadron at Conningsby are prepared for a 5½-hour transit flight from Cyprus to the UK. The large underwing fuel tanks are not carried during gun firing sorties.

Opposite: Flying in close formation whilst looking directly into sun can be tricky. By moving your aircraft up or down slightly it's possible to hide the lead aircraft in front of the sun, producing an unusual photographic effect.

Below: 763, a Royal Saudi Arabian Tornado GR 1 in full desert camouflage, one of forty-eight ordered by the Saudi government. This aircraft belongs to 7 Squadron based at Dharan air base.

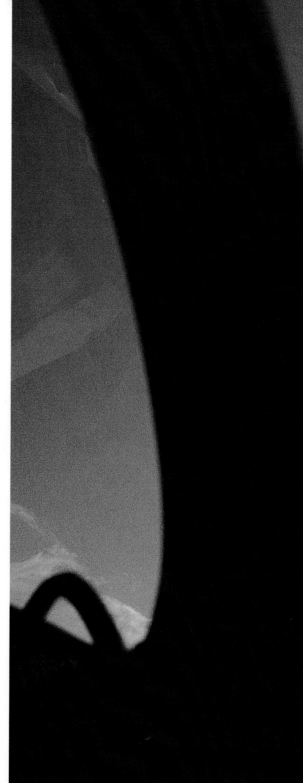

Opposite: Ground crew examine the extended Frazer Nash
launcher used to push the Skyflash missile away from the
fuselage prior to motor burn.

Below: Early morning light glints off two Red Eagle Tornado F3s.

Opposite: Posing for the camera, the first four Royal Saudi Air Force Tornado F3s on their delivery flight, accompanied by a Tristar of 216 Squadron.

Below: Six Tornados from 25(F) Squadron fly an immaculate formation on the day the Squadron number was officially announced as 25. The Squadron has a long tradition of formation flying dating back to the 1930s, when it took part in the annual Hendon Air Days.

Overleaf: A clean (no weapons fitted) Tornado GR 1 from 36 Stormo based at Gioia del Colle in Italy. The Aeronautics Militare Italiana (AMI) operate 100 ground attack Tornados.

Opposite: Flt Lt Watson, a 20 Squadron Tornado GR 1 pilot, lowers the canopy prior to taxi. Once the canopy is lowered, both crew have the luxury of a Martin Baker Mk10 ejector seat with a zero-zero capability, e.g. at zero feet and zero speed or simply stationery on the ground.

Below: Colourful fins: the white fin of D-A, a 31 Squadron Tornado GR 1, is obviously showing signs of heavy reverse thrust use.

Opposite: 'O' Oscar, a 2 Squadron Tornado GR 1, kicks in the reheat. 2 Squadron have by tradition allocated the tail letters S-H-I-N-Y- T-W-O E-R- to their aircraft.

Below: With its wings swept aft, the Tornado F3 is probably the fastest low-level aircraft in the NATO inventory. Speeds well in excess of 750 knots at 250 feet have been recorded during development flying. High level performance is in excess of Mach 2.

Opposite: Kit from Tornado GR 1. One of the major advantages of the Tornado is the accessibility of equipment located behind the many panels along the fuselage side.

Below: With Tattershall Castle as a back drop, the place can only be RAF Conningsby, home of 229 OCU, 5 and 29 Squadrons.

Opposite: Holding the echelon starboard position, two Tornado F3s cruise the North Sea, their normal area of operations.

Below: Having completed a two versus two DACT (Dissimilar Air Combat Training) mission, a pair of 17(F) Squadron Tornado GR 1s are escorted back to RAF Leeming by a Tornado F3 of 25(F) Squadron. After landing the crew would spend at least one hour reconstructing and debriefing the mission.

Overleaf: Parked outside its hardened aircraft shelter, E-Q, a
dual control trainer of 23 Squadron is readied for another sortie.

Opposite: A German air force Tornado GR 1 performs a steep
climbing turn immediately after take-off. Just visible are the
Kreuger flaps. Not fitted on RAF aircraft, these are small flaps on
the wing nib just forward of the wing sweep area.

Below: 'In close'.

Opposite: Alongside the tug, Canberras provide a sterling task in towing the air-to-air banners used for air gunnery. Each banner is six feet by thirty feet, although I'm sure it shrinks when airborne.

Below: *ZE729*, a comparatively rare bird, was operated by the Tornado Operational Evaluation unit at Coningsby and is flown here by Squadron Leaders Paddy O'Flyn and Andy Lister-Tomlinson. The aircraft is carrying a single AIM 9 L Sidewinder missile on its port wing pylon.

Opposite: En route to the play area: a 617 GR 1, complete with practice bombs, heads out to sea prior to a four versus four versus four affiliation sortie against F15 Eagles and Tornado F3s.

Below: A Saudi Tornado F3 shines in the early morning sun.

Overleaf: The final conflict. A Lightning Mk 6 breaks away from a
Tornado F3 of the same squadron prior to a one versus one
dissimilar air combat engagement.

Opposite: The 'Sharp End' — looking into the front seat of a 229
OCU Tornado F3. Dominating the centre windscreen is the Head
Up Display (HUD) system. This shows the pilot a multitude of
information from weapon symbology and attack steering to
aircraft speed, angle of attack and altitude.

Below: Mission Accomplished.

Opposite: Unusual rear shot of a Tornado GR 1 showing off its two RB199 jet pipes. In the centre is the gearing which allows the thrust reverse buckets to deploy during the landing run.

Below: Mixed fins, RAF Leeming 1989. Left to right: D-L, 31 Squadron; B-A, 14 Squadron, and D-J, 11 Squadron.

Opposite: Silhouette against the sun, an Air Defence Tornado hugs my wing for a close formation recovery into RAF Valley.

Below: *Z904 AE*, an F2 of 229 OCU, displays the original red and yellow flash on the nose prior to the unit adopting the markings of 65 (Reserve) Squadron.

Opposite: A fully loaded Tornado GR 1 of 617 Squadron (the Dambusters) banks away, wings swept back for a high speed dash.

Below: Mounted on the opposite side to that of the Tornado F3, the Tornado GR 1 sits with its bolt-on in-flight refuelling probe in the fully extended position.

Opposite: With its wings swept back at sixty-seven degrees, E-B
of 23 Squadron accelerates up into the cold upper air.

Below: In wartime, UK-based Tornado GR 1s would increase
their range by the use of in-flight refuelling from Victor, VC10 or
Tristar Tankers.

Opposite: On CAP (Combat Air Patrol), a fully loaded Tornado F3 from 11 Squadron pulls into a tight left turn at around 400 mph and 2000 feet. The pilot, Sqn Ldr Paul Burnside, was the first to achieve 1000 hours solely on the Tornado F3.

Below: 27 Squadron are based alongside 617 Squadron at RAF Marham in Norfolk. Visible under the nose is the laser target designator encased in a glass mount.

Opposite: Awaiting its crew, a Tornado F3 sites inside a HAS (Hardened Aircraft Shelter). Two aircraft are normally stored in each shelter, along with large stocks of spares, weapons and fuel tanks. In times of tension these shelters would be home to both air crew and ground crew alike.

Below: The two-man crew close the canopy of this 20 Squadron machine prior to starting the left engine. Unlike the Air Defence variant, Ground Attack Tornados have two internally mounted 27 mm cannons, one mounted either side of the radome.

Opposite: Plugged into a VC10 of 101 Squadron based at RAF Brize Norton in Oxfordshire. The small white 'beta' lights around the edge of the basket form a white circle to ease air-to-air refuelling at night.

Below: Unusual mixed formation of German Navy and former German Navy aeroplanes, led by the Seahawk of the Royal Navy's Historic Flight and flanked by two F104 Starfighters with two Tornado GR 1s in the rear.

Opposite: A familiar coastal landmark, Flamborough Head, provides the backdrop for the 11 Squadron flagship, Delta Hotel. At slow speed and heavy weight the rear slab stabilator is angled downwards to maintain the aircraft's climb angle.

Below: 25(F) Squadron's Foxtrot-Hotel searches the upper air above a thick blanket of cumulus cloud.

Opposite: Their grey camouflage blending into an overcast background, two 25 Squadron Tornado F3s fly a loose stepped echelon formation with wings swept fully aft.

Below: *ZE858 F-K* of ? Squadron. The question mark was applied to the fin prior to a decision being made regarding the third and final RAF Leeming Squadron.

Opposite: One of the most essential factors in air-to-air photography is strong sunlight. I have moved the aircraft to allow it to be front lit as opposed to side lit. This accentuates the sleek lines in the wings swept position.

Below: Tornado prototype PO 4 98+05 in its attractive red, white and black colour scheme. At this stage the aircraft was known as the Multi Role Combat Aircraft.

Opposite: With its two MK104 RB199s in full combat power, D-G of 11 Squadron, loaded with two external ferry tanks, starts its take-off role.

Below: Arabian tails. Two Saudi Arabian Tornado GR 1s pause for a refuel during their delivery flight in May 1987.

Opposite: Upper view of 17(F) Squadron's specially painted aircraft. The black zig-zag markings are reminiscent of the time when the squadron flew Bristol Bulldogs in the 1930s.

Below: Detail of a 14 Squadron Tornado GR 1. The Squadron must hold the record for the length of time it has been based abroad. Since the late 1940s 14 Squadron have been Germany based. Its present station, RAF Bruggen on the Dutch/German border, is the RAF's largest Tornado base.

Opposite: *ZE209* of 229 OCU was originally delivered to 29 Squadron prior to its transfer. The conversion unit aircraft bears the markings of 65 Squadron (a reserve unit), a number they would adopt in time of tension.

Below: Looking faded after five weeks of blazing sunshine, three 5 Squadron Tornado F3s line up on RAF Akrotiri's main runway. With the long range ferry tanks fitted, singleton take-offs are normally the order of the day.

Overleaf: Three Tornado GR 1s from 20 Squadron fly a close
arrow formation across the Vale of Pickering in Yorkshire. Each
aircraft carries two 1500 litre under-wing fuel tanks, a Skyshadow
jamming pod and a Phillips BOZ 107 chaff and flare dispenser
(starboard wing). Also carried for self defence are Sidewinder
air-to-air missle rails, above the 1500 litre tanks.

Opposite: Low over the Baltic, a German Marineflieger Tornado
GR 1 leads an RAF Tornado F3 interceptor back to base.
(Photograph S. Black)

Below: Many crews who fly in the air defence role prefer white
flying helmets, which supposedly reflect heat from strong
sunlight at high altitude. Low level Tornado GR 1 crews always
use green to avoid detection.

Opposite: This aircraft is aptly coded Delta-Hotel, a term used by bomber pilots when scoring a direct hit. High on the tail is the gold star denoting a machine from 31 Squadron, 'The Gold Stars'.

Below: Flight Lieutenant I D McDonald-Webb, a former Lightning pilot, climbs *ZE833* into the evening sky.

Overleaf: 'Breaking out'.

Opposite: Silhouette of E-C, a 23 Squadron Tornado F3.

Below: Over wintry fields three 20 Squadron Tornado GR 1s
head back to Germany, having flown a low level mission in the
Lake District. Flying this close is not a normal tactical formation.

Opposite: Inside the aircraft servicing hanger at RAF Leeming *ZE858* is accepted from the British Aerospace factory at Warton on to RAF strength.

Below: Italian Tornado GR 1 shows its colourful yellow lightning tail flash.

Opposite: Mission accomplished, a Tornado GR 1 crew dismount. Internal ladders are not fitted to any Tornados.

Below: 'MacRobert's Reply' 'F' of XV (15) Squadron based at Laarbruch in West Germany. The story dates from World War 2 when Lady MacRobert donated a Sterling bomber to the RAF in memory of her three sons killed whilst flying. The Sterling *N6068* F-Freddie flew with 15 Squadron from October 1941 to January 1942. During this period it took part in the unsuccessful raid to bomb the Tirpitz in the Trondheim fjord. F-Freddie carried the MacRobert family crest on its nose, along with the inscription 'MacRobert's Reply'. Today a single Tornado GR 1, like the Buccaneers before it, carries the same inscription.

Opposite: Over a typical North Yorkshire scene, this Tornado F3 lacks its two inboard Sidewinder missiles. The normal fit is four Skyflash and four Sidewinder air missiles.

Below: A close up of *ZE809* E-Z of 23 Squadron.

Opposite: Sitting on the runway's end, an F3 runs up its engines
to fifty per cent reheat prior to brake release.

Below: G Force 'pulling G'.

Opposite: PO 3 *XX947*, the first British MRCA (Tornado) to fly. The circular roundel on the fin comprises the three nations involved in the programme, Britain, Italy and Germany.

Below: Although shown in colours of the German Marineflieger, 98+05 is actually prototype P04. The rear cockpit is covered, either to conceal classified equipment or covering test equipment. Some of the early aircraft were flown with one pilot only, the rear seat being filled with instrumentation equipment.

Opposite: Plan view showing the variable geometry wings fully aft. One of the most frequently asked questions is 'What happens to the underwing stores when the wings sweep?' The pylons are synchronized to move with the wings as they sweep forward and back. It is easy to see from this angle that the drop tanks are adjacent to the rear stabilators.

Below: Sleek Fighter.

Opposite: Flaps are set to the mid-position for normal Tornado F3 take-offs, giving the clean aircraft a respectably short take-off roll.

Below: Another prototype, *ZA267*, is an ADV (Air Defence Variant). To be exact, this was the second ADV prototype — the first flew on 27 October 1979. This ADV, sen at the Greenham Common airshow, has several unusual features: the fuel tanks are three finned; the asterisk symbols along the fuselage and tail are used for telemetry, and the fin has a forward-facing camera fitted.

Overleaf: Flying line astern, CC of the then newly formed 5
Squadron, formates on a Tornado F3 of 229 OCU.

Opposite: Detailed view of a Saudi Tornado GR 1. The gun barrel
has been blanked off for the delivery flight.

Below: *ZE735*, a dual control Tornado F3, was originally
delivered to 5 Squadron at RAF Conningsby on 2 February 1988.
By June 1989 it was moved to 25(F) Squadron, becoming FE, seen
here three weeks later.

Opposite: Lieutenant Colonel Urbano, Italian Air Force, Commander of 155 Stormo based at Gehdi in Northern Italy, runs through his pre-start checks.

Below: This Italian Tornado seems to have more markings on it than camouflage. The number *X-587* on the fin indicates an early aircraft. The cockpit front and back also seems devoid of instruments and ejector seats.

SALVATAGGIO
RESCUE
IM NOTFALL

MANIGLIA EMERGENZA
FRANTUMAZ. TETTUCCIO
SULL' ALTRO LATO

EMERGENCY ENTRANCE
CONTROL ON OTHER SIDE

NOTGRIFF ZUM AUFSPRENGEN
DER KABINENDACHVERGLASUNG
AUF DER ANDEREN SEITE

DANGER
DO NOT PULL
HANDLE

Overleaf: Tanking in thick cloud, as seen here, can be a disorientating exercise. The Tornado's two-man crew can prove invaluable in such situations with the navigator passing the pilot reassuring attitude information.

Opposite: Alongside the flying petrol tanker, the pilot sites abeam the VC10's window with his probe extended, indicating a need to refuel. The Tanker captain will then trial his hoses if fuel is available.

Below: 'Bavarian Bomber', a German Air Force Tornado GR 1, painted in a traditional Bavarian blue and white scheme with patriotic yellow, red and black radome, is celebrating fifty years of Jabo G32, based at Lechfeld.

Opposite: 17(F) Squadron Special Tornado GR 1 C-Z skims across solid cloud. Unusually for Germany-based Tornados, it is fitted with a bolt-on refuelling probe.

Below: Waiting for a range slot, three live-armed Tornado F3s skip through scattered cloud off the west Welsh coast.

Opposite: June 1988 — one of the last sorties flown by 11(F) Squadron as a Lightning unit. Wg Cdr D Hamilton escorts *XR754* B-C for this unique event. In keeping with tradition, 11 Squadron kept the rectangular fighter bars on the nose of their new mounts.

Below: 44+13, a German single stick Tornado GR 1, number 77 of an order for 394, taxies for its maiden flight at Manching, S. Germany.

Opposite: The black fin and spine of this 11 Squadron Tornado make it the most colourful Tornado F3 so far.

Below: Tornado F3 from RAF Leeming over familiar territory, the North Yorkshire moors.

Opposite: The sleek lines of the Air Defence Variant are shown to its advantage here. With its wings swept back at sixty-seven degrees, the ground technician prepares to attach a cable to the arrester hook and winch the Tornado F3 back into its hardened shelter.

Below: 2 ATAF (Allied Tactical Air Force) ops. A Tornado F3 from 25(F) Squadron sits in a revetment at RAF Bruggen, having flown a mission against Germany-based Tornado GR 1s of 31 Squadron.

Opposite: E-F of 23 Squadron, surrounded by essential ground equipment used for loading the Skyflash radar guided missile. The eight missile fins used for guidance are only fitted once the missile has been loaded to the aircraft.

Below: Despite a general toning down of Air Force colours and markings, it's still difficult to avoid 'glint'. Often, your position can be given away visually as you turn, because the sun reflects off your paintwork.

Opposite: A ground technician prepares an F3 for another sortie. Prior to right engine start, the aircraft is supplied by ground electrical power via the orange cable fitted aft of the radome.

Below: In the approach configuration, D-H simulates a wing sweep failure. *ZE764* maintains a speed around 230 knots for a swept wing approach — fortunately, wing sweep failures are rare.

Opposite: Breaking out of close formation.

Below: Venting fuel from the fin dump outlet, an F3 glints in the midday sun.

Opposite: Whilst four of their aircraft were participating in 'Exercise Golden Eagle', a round the world tour, two aircraft from 29 Squadron set off on a more mundane mission. 'Golden Eagle' lasted sixty-six days circumnavigating the globe.

Below: 'Swing wing symmetry'.

Overleaf: Pilot's eye-view from the front cockpit of a Tornado F3, showing the twin glass head up display and its various controls.

Opposite: F-E in the sixty-seven degree wing configuration, allowing it to maintain 750 knots at 250 feet and in excess of Mach 2 at high level. Powered by two Rolls-Royce RB199 three shaft multi-role engines, RB199s have exceeded one million flying hours. They produce 8000 lb in dry thrust and over 16,000 lb in reheat. Tornado F3s are fitted with the Mk 104 engines producing an extra seven per cent thrust over the 103s.

Below: The Tornado GR 1's rear cockpit is dominated by two TV screens and a centrally mounted moving map display unit, which can be used in conjunction with the mapping radar. The small white buttons below the TV screens are the multi function keyboards used to vary the information displayed to the navigator.

Below: Night cap: a pair of Tornado F3s and a Hawk T1a set off on an evening intercept mission.